821 DOO

3 821 DOO

LEARNING. services

01209 616259

Cornwall College Camborne
Learning Centre - FE

This resource is to be returned on or before the last date stamped below. To renew items please contact the Centre

Three Week Loan

D1333504

101457

CORNWALL COLLEGE
LIBRARY

MAURA DOOLEY

Sound Barrier

POEMS 1982-2002

BLOODAXE BOOKS

Copyright © Maura Dooley
1986, 1988, 1991, 1996, 2002

ISBN: 1 85224 578 6

First published 2002 by
Bloodaxe Books Ltd,
Highgreen,
Tarset,
Northumberland NE48 1RP.

www.bloodaxebooks.com
For further information about Bloodaxe titles
please visit our website or write to
the above address for a catalogue.

Bloodaxe Books Ltd acknowledges
the financial assistance of Northern Arts.

LEGAL NOTICE
All rights reserved. No part of this book may be
reproduced, stored in a retrieval system, or
transmitted in any form, or by any means, electronic,
mechanical, photocopying, recording or otherwise,
without prior written permission from Bloodaxe Books Ltd.
Requests to publish work from this book
must be sent to Bloodaxe Books Ltd.
Maura Dooley has asserted her right under
Section 77 of the Copyright, Designs and Patents Act 1988
to be identified as the author of this work.

Cover printing by J. Thomson Colour Printers Ltd, Glasgow.

Printed in Great Britain by
Cromwell Press Ltd, Trowbridge, Wiltshire.

For David

Acknowledgements

This book includes all the poems which Maura Dooley wishes to keep in print from her collections *Ivy Leaves & Arrows* (Bloodaxe Books, 1986), *Turbulence* (Giant Steps, 1988), *Explaining Magnetism* (Bloodaxe Books, 1991) and *Kissing a Bone* (Bloodaxe Books, 1996), together with a group of new poems. The first two sections include some poems later reprinted in *Explaining Magnetism*, while *Moss* combines poems from *Explaining Magnetism* and *Kissing a Bone*, with the addition of a pair of later poems, 'Casey, Cullen, Ward and McKeogh, 1969' and 'Casey, Cullen and Ward, 1999', and *The Future Memory* is a sequence originally published in *Kissing a Bone*.

Acknowledgements are due to the editors of the following publications in which some of the new poems, or versions of the new poems, first appeared: *The Guardian, Kunapipi, The Independent on Sunday, Last Words: New Poetry for the New Century* (Picador, 1999), *Mslexia, Moving Worlds, New Writing 6, The North, Poetry Review* and *The Waiting Room*.

'1943' and 'The Blackbird Whistling' were commissioned by BBC Radio 3 for the Proms 2000. 'Invitations on the Mantlepiece' was originally commissioned in another form by BBC Radio 4 for the series *Better Than Sex*. 'Rafts of Desires' and 'Our Lives and Ourselves' were commissioned by Midlands Arts Centre and the Irish Arts Council. 'Raft of Desires' now exists as a permanent installation on Ryde Pier, Isle of Wight.

Contents

Moss

The Future Memory

Are they assigned, or can the countries pick their colors?
– What suits the character or the native waters best.
Topography displays no favorites; North's as near as West.
More delicate than the historians' are the map-makers colors.

ELIZABETH BISHOP: 'The Map'

FROM

IVY LEAVES & ARROWS

Visiting

Watching the soapy swill trickle away,
cloudy in soft water, a scum on hard,
glittering over Armitage Shanks
or Twyford's Vitreous Enamel.
And from the window a mountain,
a back wall, a square of blue sky somewhere,
through net, through frosted glass,
through an open window. Visiting.

Trying to imagine how it would be
to live out this life, I have
loitered by estate agents' windows
and done up that old shack in spare weekends.
But in these distant friendly bathrooms,
though I use your soap and borrow towels,
my toothbrush rests uneasy on the shelf.

A Small Shaking of My Picture of the Kingdom

A small shaking of my picture of the kingdom;
counters jarred a little, down a tiny snake

or up a ladder. A straightening of spectacles,
a new page in the road atlas, women at a bus-stop,

more red brick or narrow lanes, a going-home of schools,
a blue or yellow bus, somewhere in England.

Against it all I shore what makes this home,
wide light, a weaver's window, each stone in that wall.

This is the heart's small change,
a little silver saved against the rain.

Even That Routine

The roof is lipped with milk.
Never before such brightness,
so much of it, mulled here
by winter sun and hawthorn shadow
to the lightest cream.
Cooling, it forms a skin on my world,
sits like a thatch on my slates,
loops low over the bedroom window
a sail taut against the blue wind.

When you had wrung every drop from her,
playing plain course gently, lightly,
I stood above the silvery pail,
milk lapping its sides,
longing to plunge my arms
into its feathery wet warmth.

Bored with even that routine
you sold her. Now the ice knits,
now the snow thickens
around her locked and silent shed.
It's cold and in the dusty pail
we carry in coal for our fire.

Six Filled the Woodshed with Soft Cries

From grass-stained eggs we bred eight;
two hens, six fine white cockerels,
they scrambled, fluffing feathers,
for a summer and an autumn month.

Now, hands pinked by the wind,
I watch their maned necks nervously.
Yesterday the tiniest learnt to crow,
latched a strange voice to crisp air,
his blood red comb fluting the wind,
feathers creaming, frothing at his throat.

One month till Christmas, the clouds thicken,
he turns on me an icy, swivel eye,
Do you dare deny me?

My neighbour helps me chase them,
snorting snuff, which rests on his sleeve
in a fine white scatter. A wicker basket
gapes wide as he dives for them.

Six filled the woodshed with soft cries.
Their feathers cover stony ground
like a lick of frost.

Over the Fields

Whoever heard of a seamless garment?
This is a sky scabby with stars,
a moon that eats a hole in the grass,
a night announced by the drone of a plane
and lit by tail lights.

There's owl screech and fox-bark,
wake them and the geese will laugh
blisters to your face.
But the phone still rings,
the television flickers,
over the fields wires hum.

Towards Summer

The ferns are making a fist of spring,
punching the dark valley green.
Our minds turn again to painting
and patching. We should mend the weather vane:

four arrows, flightless, aimed at hill
and sky. Two letters are missing,
but *S* and *W* point towards summer
and only zephyrs are welcomed here.

What would we gain by restoring *N* and *E*?
A Pole Star, harsh winds, *NEWS*.
In a surprising spring we can forget
about the papers, doze in the sun

under a broken weather vane,
imagining it might always be like this.

The Women of Mumbles Head

The moon is sixpence,
a pillar of salt or
a shoal of herring.
But on such a night,
wild as the wet wind,
larger than life,
she casts a long line
over the slippery sea.
And the women of Mumbles Head
are one, a long line,
over the slippery sea.
Wet clothes clog them,
heavy ropes tire them,
but the women of Mumbles Head
are one, a long line,
over the slippery sea.
And under white beams
their strong arms glisten,
like silver, like salt,
like a shoal of herring,
under the slippery sea.
And they haul
for their dear ones,
and they call
for their dear ones,
casting a long line
over the slippery sea.
But the mounting waves
draw from them,
the mountain waves
draw from them,
the bodies of their dear ones,
O, the bodies of their dear ones,
drawn under the slippery sea.

In a chain of shawls
they hook one in,
fish-wet, moonlit,
they've plucked him back
from under the slippery sea.
For the moon is sixpence,
a pillar of salt
or a shoal of herring,
and the women of Mumbles Head
are one, a long line
over the slippery sea.

The women rescued a lifeboatman by making
a rope of their knotted shawls, after the
Mumbles lifeboat was lost in a storm in 1883.

Early Morning

The garden
rising
from its bed
of frost
is green
as a raw glass
swilled
with faint colour,
crude sparkle.
I run my eyes
around its rim
and hear it ring.

Gypsophila Paniculata

What do they call this? Like ice or lace,
its whitest petal is not as pale as you
nor each thin stem as fragile. A florist's flower
it hangs from bridal hands, a summer dust.
But when you could no longer cloud a glass
they laid it round your tiny box like smoke,
and villagers' flowers, imperfect, bright,
filled borrowed jugs and vases while
that frosted candy fizzed its saddest jest,
Gypsophila Paniculata, Baby's Breath.

An Exile

Blaubeeren,
a bloom, a taste of sap rising,
risen maybe, and wood and green shade.
We made syrup and jam
and it was like Alice's drink,
a sort of mixed flavour of cherry tart,
custard, pineapple, hot buttered toast,
everything nice you can possibly think of.

But best was that smoke sweetness,
fresh from its light green bush
rolled from cheek to cheek,
and our tongues long and blue.
In London we bought them in jars,
Polish, deep dark with promise,
and once, in such a smart shop,
I found them fresh and they cost –
were so expensive – and I carried
them home, like glass, or a prize,
their cardboard cradle blurred with juice.
I heaped white china bowls with them,
relished the stains that bled on the cloth.
So it was bitter to taste the dust,
the cool blandness of them,
and my heart wept.

Ah, but I ate each one slowly,
stared deep in the mirror,
to step back I sighed, step through.
I looked hard at my tongue, long, tied, silent,
I looked hard at my tongue,
and saw it was blue.

Sugar Frosting

His small hard mouth
is flushed with fruit,
his breath is sweet
with stolen strawberries,
he blows a dust of candy
on your neck, a sugar frosting,
and through it bites your flesh.
Down on the damp grass,
through a tangle of leaves,
his hands stir and plunder.
The cheek you turn to him
is downy with pale hair,
stippled with freckles,
a Seurat of strawberry and rose.

CORNWALL COLLEGE
LIBRARY

Questions You Can't Answer

It used to be the highest mountain
or the nearest planet. Holding the fruit
between thumb and finger you told me
the earth is not round, the earth is not flat.
But why a blood orange? You sighed.
Laid your knife on a plate where crescents
of peel were leaning, offering up their fat
gondolas as your pared world.

                        And by now
I've learnt how to cut to the right depth,
how to prise my fingers between the segments
which pull free, falling pale, diminished, pithy.
The thin skin of the fruit is streaked bloody
and, always clumsy, my hands run with juice.

Before me in the queue a nervous woman asks,
'Are those South African oranges?'
Smiling, he shakes his head.
'I know what you mean love, don't worry, we like
to know who's had their paws on them, don't we?'

FROM

TURBULENCE

Green Man

He will ask too much,
come into the bright shade
of longing and want too much.
Outside, the sun blinds us with
spring, he will draw the leaves
from the trees and into this house
where white walls cool us and
he will see too much,
come into the clean sheets
of longing and know too much.
Outside, the birds drown us with
song, he will draw the story
from the stream and into this house
where stone floors chill us and
he will need too much,
come into the dry mouth
of longing and ask too much.

Wedding Guest

In the photograph he pulls
from his hired-suit pocket
we are younger. I am surprised
by his ease, by his charm,
as I see him surprised by mine.
While we assure each other
that we'll meet again soon,
he spreads out on the table
some laughter, a past, and
something I can't quite see.
It is held in smooth brown hands,
held in hands I remember.

Emperors of Ice Cream

and bid them whip
In kitchen cups concupiscent curds.
WALLACE STEVENS

Once Neapolitan striped our Sundays,
or butter yellow glazed a silver dish,
on Weston sands a cardboard Wallsiwhip
and logs of chocolate, in their makeshift shed,
beckoned cautious summer to your open hands.

Years before, D'Ambrosio drew ice by horse
through a salty town, delicious and slow.
Each May his daughters, decked with flowers,
sailed into the teeming church, like swans,
till he folded his apron to rest with the linen,
pressed like a cake of soap or block of ice
flawless, amongst dried orange blossom,
waiting for the war to end.

And now, drawn by a tray and sparkling coat
we slide down milky dunes, a tiny bell
summoning us to a communion of coolness:
split by bananas, rippled with raspberries,
dappled by sand, we tongue with eagerness.

In Italy she saw a small miracle,
a green-veined pip in lemon water ice,
and she has to believe in it now, she knows it's real.
Back here the Capaldis, Minghellas and Verrecchias
of summer colour our landscape,
we have painted our sturdy villas softly,
the pinks and peppermints of sorbets or
the creamy yellows of a vanilla cone.

And when it rains in Fortes the wicker creaks,
those green and gold and glass-topped tables
float fluted dishes, fan-tailed wafers,
and spoons that never can quite reach
the end of a glory that is knickerbockerless.

Up on the Moors with Keeper

Three girls under the sun's rare brilliance
out on the moors, hitching their skirts
over bog-myrtle and bilberry.

They've kicked up their heels at a dull brother
whose *keep still can't you?* wants to fix
them to canvas. Emily's dog stares at these

three girls under the juggling larks
pausing to catch that song on a hesitant wind,
all wings and faces dipped in light.

What could there be to match this glory?
High summer, a scent of absent rain,
away from the dark house, father and duty.

Shadow on Her Desk

A year after the courtroom heard those tapes
I'm running through the dark blue evening,
October fires keen on the wind, winter quickening.

In the tightening of fingers and the tightening of rules
something terrible was being hidden from us,
only the fear passed on, in rumour, safe at school.

Never take sweets from strangers (I'm running).
Don't accept lifts from people you don't know.
Better to be safe than sorry (I'm running).

That Friday I burst into a house doused with fish
my mother busy cooking, my father shushing me,
full of all my news my father shuts me up.

But I am shut before he says it,
seeing him crying, staring at the telly, crying.
Coal that burns in our grate has shut them up.

A slag heap, a tip, a shadow on her desk,
safe at school it shut them in the ground.
Safe at school it shut them.

After twenty years the one they tugged clear
stares out beyond the whirr of cameras
to the valley. Children gone, work gone,

only the green and the rain keep returning.
Fir trees are planted on man-made hills,
they've put up a memorial in pale cement.

After twenty years we are raking over old coals
but something terrible is being hidden from us,
only the fear passed on, in rumour, safe at school.

Don't play outside today (I'm crying).
Wash all green-leaved vegetables thoroughly.
Don't drink rainwater (I'm crying).

Saddleworth, Aberfan, Chernobyl: a kind of litany.
Up on the wet green moor police start to dig.

Banging the Bomb

I wanted to know why they had
to bang the Bomb. Mum explained
what ban meant, but under the bed
the man with no legs was waiting
to get me, his crate smashed in the Drink
and his tin legs locked up. My nightmares
were full of the explosion, his stumps.

One screaming night my mum held
my hand, told me of her father's old trench
coat, the bone she had felt in its lining,
the dreams of skull, blood, gas and mud,
how, years later, still trembling, she drew
from that deep pocket a briar pipe,
sweet tobacco dry and meek in its bowl.

But now this child feels the bone beneath
her mattress, hears something beyond
the wind's sighing. They can't find words
to comfort her, at breakfast try hard to be
ordinary, smile brightly, turn on the radio,
wish it wasn't the news again.

Missiles Over Buxton

On the ridge road down through windy Derbyshire,
watching trees shake themselves in a mild autumn
I see a devil's fork rise into sleepy cloud.

Lights in the sky: a gently arcing evil.
When I ask *what is it?* my heart is plunging
into downy silence. Surely it must be a dream?

This year we are trawling Halley's comet,
other times I've fished for falling stars and
hoped I'd never catch this nameless terror.

In a second's hour of silence, before your safe reply,
I see my mother's face, aunty Kitty's neat back garden,
my father's hair, your eyes, your hands.

A moment's strangeness tricked us: the half light,
the greenness, no other car on this long damp road,
under the thinning trees, the clouds, the radio masts.

Later in Buxton Opera House, I tilt borrowed glasses at the cherubs.
They crease rosy cheeks, flash gilded wings,
cross dimpled thighs, wreathing the stage with joy.

Outside, above the hills of windy Derbyshire,
stars dance between those radio masts, a comet nears,
the air waves glitter with important messages.

Eating Out

When you turned up suddenly
with flowers and wine, we ate out,
finding only sardines in the dark
cupboard. We swished through the damp
streets, parked the car neatly, to cut up
problems on someone else's tablecloth.

Days later I toss the roses
in the bin. Three hundred miles away,
almost home, the untouched claret
rolls round on your back seat
like some memory: Greenham.

You slow the car beside a knot
of cold women, a tiny fire, their serious
faces, *thank you*, you say, in tears,
clumsily handing over the bottle at last.

No Harvest

News of your mother's death
reaches me like someone
shifting furniture upstairs,
dull thunder on an autumn evening.

– for the smell of her to fade –
I phone with nothing to say.

My own mother, miles away,
stirs sloes we picked together
rocking them slightly in a sea
of gin, bruising them bloodier daily.

Despite squeezing and prodding,
a needle purified in candle flame,
our hands are studded still with
hedgerow scars, thorn ends lodged

just under our similar skins.
– for the smell of her to fade –

This is no harvest: the clouds
sudden collusion to let in winter,
a turning back of clocks to no effect.
Needing to gather-in some comfort

not finding it in woods or fields,
among berries, I syphon off that
deepening bruise, wanting to share
with you a distillation of love.

FROM

EXPLAINING MAGNETISM

Out

It's a medieval life
in this country's great capital.

Bloodied glass and bone and bile.
Wounds nursed beneath the stars:

we're out all night, every night,
under that distant glitter,

bandaged up with promise
and that old anaesthetic, hope.

The streets yield up their dead
alive, loused up, leaky,

dancing till dawn
in ball-gowns or rags;

is it greed honed to a mean
sharp-tongued conclusion,

this chorus of more, more, more
and a choreographed turning of backs?

Or just another kind of quickstep
through centuries of silence

with all the ancient arms presented,
fists, iron, stone.

Mind the Gap

We have settled on either side of a bridge, under arches,
medieval, Dickensian or twentieth-century. Over the bridge
a flutter of commuters, under the bridge the Thames,
beside the bridge a nest of survivors in cardboard.
Heading North, at night, with a suitcase and new coat
you hear rats in the Underground scratching over what's left,
a recorded voice   calling   Mind the Gap   Mind the Gap.

That swift, sad jump is replayed second by second
in the corner of your eye. But why today when sunlight
made the river almost lovely? Perhaps because it put him
beyond stomach pump or reason and when the sun
came out he was blinded by sorrow, hung up like sheets
for the wind to fill, billowing out over London, gathering dirt.
O take him down, bring him in, bundle him up in time,

before the clouds gather, before the rain comes.

Success

The man with the Tesco bag is still out there.
He spends each day crossing, recrossing, the busy street.

Yes, I'll find it, he is muttering, *just show me where it is.*
Where is it? Where is it? Look how dazzling his shirt is,

how neat his hair, he hasn't pissed himself, he isn't dirty
but he stinks of the thing we all dread most. You write to me

about success as if it was something to do with an odourless
accent, or years of wearing wholesomeness next to the skin,

or holding up the amulet of niceness. It's a fairy circle
appearing overnight, out of the dark its pale dome growing

but it's only fungus, a frail stalk in muck. From where I stand
you are the very face of it, someone who learnt to say *no*.

Over the babycall you catch her sobbing.
Juana, the Brazilian nanny, is sobbing
sobbing, sobbing: her heart in her mouth
heaving her, heavy in her.
In the café Fernando gathers up plates,
stacking them in the sink as orderly
as once he lined up books in his Rio study.
In half a dozen bathrooms Maria scrubs
at basins till under scum and elbowgrease
she almost sees herself. Or is it her mother?

What seemed like a chance or choice,
a way out, a new start, luck,
clothes them now as all there is.
They could die here at an early age, or older,
having found a pleasant flat to rent, or not,
watching the days pile up like plates or nappies,
swilling our dirt away with consummate care,
making it all look nice, washing it all away.

Office

At night your sleep is a race
down dimly lit passages where
the floor shines up at you,
the corridor never ends.

Each time you're searching
for the office door but when
you find it, it's stuck fast
and through the toughened glass

you can make it all out:
the windows nailed shut,
the phones chirruping,
the desks piled high with paper.

Awake, your eyes feel starched open
and rushing for the number 19 or 5
you check your head for a showercap,
check your feet for slippers.

You join the lift's
conspiracy of silence,
its collision of Chanels,
numbers 19 and 5.

Between coffees and invoices,
questions gather in the in-tray,
are dismissed in the out-tray,
resolved in the bin.

Other people's sadnesses
blow in like dust. Your nose
and ears, your eyes and mouth
are full of them. You write letters

offering hope like a biscuit.
You pour tea to untangle the net
of your colleagues' affairs.
Fear spreads through your gut

to lodge like a knot of fury
that you suck mints to ease
and call indigestion.
You go home lonely and at night

you toss and turn, running down
a corridor that never ends.

Bee Keeping in the War Zone

The beekeeper, whose box
of pure gold hums, holds
her drowsy bees like a lantern
to soothe your sticky dreams.

She spins a sweetness into
the damp night where
you sleep badly, tossing and turning
under a flutter of green:

it's Sandino fanning you
with huge banana leaves that change
as you watch, to a shower
of banknotes. Next morning

you leave quickly, eyes stiff
with nightmare and let the
beekeeper guide you through
trees and rifles, your ears filling with

occasional gunfire, distant humming.

Romantic Encounter

You were in a plane, all propeller and thunder sheet,
only sunlight polishing the cool distance between you
and the sea flashing an innocent belly far below.

Leather fits closely about your head: brain, bone, blood ticking,
all snug as a walnut in its shell, or the cinch of silk
bunched perfectly by pale hands you dream of. *Gee Whizz.*

You are in a plane, a wind machine plays havoc with your
entrance, raindrops rattle like dried peas on the sophistication
of your dive, an elegant computerised swoop and it's *Gotcha,*

no curtains for you but heavy kisses blown at that
black shadow creeping below: skull, crossbones, blood
singing, or remembered spilt perfectly on a silk sheet

as, dimly, you imagine her pale flesh trembling,
that stain drying to the rusty shape of England.

No, Go On

For years he's gone over her parting words,
the ones she couldn't pack. They are printed

in the circles under his eyes. They come to mind
each night at 5 a.m., when the first trains start

and the moon bottles itself outside his door.
He is caught like a wheel on her shimmering track.

Over breakfast the rush hour begins and he wants
me to wait, starting another sentence that he just

lets fall away. And I'm saying: *no, go on, finish what
you were about to... I'm with you. I'm following so far.*

Drought

In the fiercest summer for years
gouts of sun sour milk in an hour,
rubbish simmers in streets which
steam with piss, swimming pools
pulse like tins of maggots
and all the time your postcards come.

Every village green turns brown,
reservoirs crack and rivers shrivel.
Each time I try to picture your face
sweat breaks over me
sudden as a storm
and all the time your postcards come.

Views of the Seine, the Tiber, the Nile,
necks of gondolas hooking through mist,
the Rhône, the Ganges, the Orinoco,
diving for danger at Acapulco.
All I ask's a screw, the shrink, a drink.
Honey, why do I always dream of death?

I can never slake this thirst,
can't eat, can't sleep, can't work, can't breathe,
my skin is scorched: the earth is tinder,
for nights I watch the hillside burn,
sparks hanging in the dark, like stars
and all the time your postcards come.

Heat silts up every artery,
the passages to my brain run dry.
Light thickens, clots, there is no shade.
Hair on my arms is bleached to straw.
You could put a match to me
but all the time, your postcards come.

Flood

Here, the bridge supports are nearly submerged
and still the tide is rising. The rain never stops.

Each time we meet there is more to say,
fewer ways of saying it. My language deepens

into hollows, there is no word for epiphany.
Every pock-mark of this shallow land is sodden,

swilling and muddied with the eddies of old storms.
I'm too old for abandonment now, too young for it.

Searching for a card for you, strung between
left blank for your own special message and

the thoughts I have for you words cannot express,
I can hear the bridge creak, the drainpipe roar.

A few rotten leaves, flushed from an autumn
hideout, sweep on along an overflowing gutter

and, eventually, I pick *Happy Birthday*. It takes me
half an hour to add, in biro, *all my love.*

Apple Pie in Pizzaland

We are apologising to one another
for our shynesses. The waitress apologises
for the lack of sultanas (not like the picture,
she says). I still probe between the slices of
apple as if I expect to find something other than
air. You spin the menu and pleat the paper napkin,
our cutlery scrapes eloquently enough.

On the train here a Canadian told me how
his province holds a lake the size of England.
I imagine you and I and Pizzaland, the green tables,
Doncaster, the fields, motorways, castles and flats,
churches, factories, corner shops, pylons, Hinkley Point,
Lands End and all of us dropped in that huge lake, *plop*.

Years later new people will stroll on
the banks, remarking how in drought
you might see the top of Centrepoint
and in the strange stillness hear the ghostly
ring and clatter of Pizzaland forks on plates.

And I'll get back to you as soon as I can

I listen to you tell why
you are not there, then dial
again to have your voice
unspool inside me, one more time.

My calls to you, like a shoal
of little wishes, replay
as clicks and silences in
the flood of business messages.

Developing a Passion

It used to be syphons and corks, a must,
a nose, stains in the linen cupboard,
a large red bucket, a deep red wine.
Now, the bathroom window blanketed,
newspaper stuffing the door black shut,
even his ears are plugged against day
and Mozart drowns her kitchen calls.
A room all dozy rose from a safety
light constant as the North Star,
a beacon, the presence of Christ.

Do you want a drink? she shouts.

His fingers puddle in search of images,
paper darkens, chemicals blush,
little miracles break out again and again.

I'm leaving your glass here, she says.

He is busy with the loaves and fishes,
forgetting wine, squinting at a reversed face,
light spills over the darkness, over and over.

How much longer are you going to be?

Her voice has an urgency he cuts with
a spinning tap. Water will sluice each flaw,
rinse away imperfection, fix truth for ever.

I won't be long, he is calling.

Downstairs she has emptied the bottle,
is weeping over a creased Polyfoto,
is burning the Man Ray, the Bailey, the Brandt.

Fundoscopy

I left the greatest masse of that unmeasurable mysterie as
a heape too heavy for my undergoing; choosing rather to walk
in a right line, than to run in a ring, whose mazefull
compasse foretells much paine with little progress.
RICHARD BANNISTER 1622 (Treatise on the eye)

You send me your first book, a text
for students, where eyes swim out of their
ken and onto the page like planets.

What is this condition? What does it tell us?

This page suggests her left eye be examined closely
with your left eye, her right eye carefully with your
right. Rest your spare hand on her forehead, it says, but

how may this affect her vision? What are these lesions?

I read on without glasses, study the plates,
confirming what I have already guessed – the adult
retina is a transparent, inelastic, multilayered tissue:

what is the solution here? What is the likely diagnosis?

When you look at me like that I want
to answer all the questions, to push my hand
behind the crystalline lens, touch a nerve.

Is this an abnormality? What causes her visual problem?

It's like a moment in that film, perhaps,
when he thinks he sees her clearly through
the two-way mirror, but she can't see him at all.

Talk

Tonight, at this party, not a face will answer,
though you half know me, and I you, remembering
the time in Capri when your voice bridged the street
disinhibited by strangeness, for weren't we friends then,
in amongst the foreign?

                    And again, in Bruxelles,
shocked out of your sense of good behaviour,
we were suddenly twinned souls in the misty city

and by the time we met in Cadiz old hands at it –
our surprise polished to buckle the belly of the world,
making it small and our own talk big. But that's all fancy.

It wasn't you I saw crossing the Place de la Piazza Plaza
that day in sunlight, it wasn't you one damp French
spring your tongue beating the cold air silver,
any more than it's you now, tilting a glass at me,
smiling cautiously, struggling to remember my name.

Letters from Yorkshire

In February, digging his garden, planting potatoes,
he saw the first lapwings return and came
indoors to write to me, his knuckles singing

as they reddened in the warmth.
It's not romance, simply how things are.
You out there, in the cold, seeing the seasons

turning, me with my heartful of headlines
feeding words onto a blank screen.
Is your life more real because you dig and sow?

You wouldn't say so, breaking ice on a waterbutt,
clearing a path through snow. Still, it's you
who sends me word of that other world

pouring air and light into an envelope. So that
at night, watching the same news in different houses,
our souls tap out messages across the icy miles.

Neighbours

We helped each other and lived in the shelter of each other.
Friendship was the fastest root in our hearts.
                    PEIG SAYERS, An Old Woman's Reflections

I'd been looking out for a loop of swallows
to tie up the end of those bitter months, when
you came carrying a litre of Chianti,
a packet of McVities Yoghurt Creams, a shovel
to bite into drifts of snow, a bag of salt to
throw at blue ice or over my shoulder
into the eyes of that devil, Winter.

Months passed, seeing your headlights cross
the valley, a low hum of engine heading home,
your washing line like a brave flag.
Spring was late, you dug through the dregs
of an old year, sawing and sowing. Things grew
and your bonfires sent more signals to me,
we're here, we're in, we're happy, busy.

It's you again today, your hands filled
with the last flowers of summer, asking me
about Yarrow. Achilles used the plant to soothe
battle wounds, daggers through the heart.
Take it, let its green fingers bind
with yours. This valley is full of it.

And know that, like the swallows, when you go
you'll leave a small vibration in the air,
a nest for some cuckoo to fill.

Backwards into Wakefield Westgate

There is a train to anywhere
and you might one day catch it.
At Mirfield, Elsenham, Bridgend or Yatton
I know you by the set of your head,
your determined walk away from me.

Why are you never on my train
which at Bradford and Wakefield
mocks the decision to face forward,
turns me round again, so I can't tell
back from front or past from future?

You look in from the other side
of carriage windows. You disappear in
the crowd at ticket barriers. I see
your cycle leaning in the guard's van.
I need you in the empty seat beside me.

The Journey Back

I stowed it all away
into a dark velvety bag,
a warm pendulous shape
under my skull. Fingering
the soft stuff of it, waiting
for the right time to unpack

a coat spun with rain and slate,
a stole threaded with bluebells,
a shawl of sunlight spangled with
black wings, a cloak the colour
of Colden Water after the thaw:
a sack full of rich raiments

its drawstring pulled tightly to
the perfect O and carried from
room to house to flat, never slackened,
spilled out or even cautiously opened.
Only at night sometimes the bag

bursts, old clothes are scattered
over valley and hill, like paths
or stepping stones, see how perfectly
they fit, how proper they would be
for such a journey – clean, comfortable,
familiar: strange as any dream.

The House Will Be Full of Dancing

That year the house was a
gift to sunlight. Antoine
threw open shutters,
propped open doors,
held open his arms to us.

For all his sweeping
dust sparkled in the
fresh air. Madame swung
the heavy windows to and fro,
testing the strength of hinges.

The quiet son arrived from Paris,
filling the house
with his mildness, but when the old
men talked to us their strange
language caught in my throat,

filled me with awkwardness,
all the sharp elbows and rough hands
of my own voice. We ran between
the rows of apple blossom
kicking up the scent like surf,

slept in rooms crackling with starch
where dust cloths were heaped up
ready for our leaving and spiders,
their silk swept away,
crouched in the cracks waiting.

A huge mirror, its gilt
tarnished, its silver faded,
bore the message of their other
English visitor, years before, XXX,
Milles Baisses scrawled in lipstick.

As we piled into the car,
Antoine prepared to lock that memory
back with the others, a chandelier,
the book that Victor Hugo
gave your Grandpapa, another
summer's herbs laid out to dry.

On imaginait là-bas, des âmes,
de belles âmes...

I imagine Madame shaking napkins
over rows of geraniums, Antoine
will loosen his shirt, lean on
his brush, smoke. I don't think of
the packing away of china

or the moths that gather for
a winter solstice. In my dream
the house will be full of dancing,
a small boy's face presses
against the pane, light will pour

from the tall windows onto his hands.

The quotation is from the final chapter
of Alain-Fournier's *Le Grand Meaulnes.*

Uncovering the Whole Thing

When they took down Redfern's Glass Works
she found a jigsaw: medieval glass, blackened,
but red beneath, rose glass for a rose window.
This was the corner where once they made jam jars,
where once a Gilbertine abbey made prayer
and between the two: the Dissolution, a river's muddy
banks, cheap housing, a warehouse and all that time
these splinters, smithereens of silica
sank themselves in earth and waited.

Sifting soil, in river mist, in drizzle,
she thought of her aunt's larder, a ray of sun
lighting up the rows of quince and bramble jelly:
jam and jars effecting a kitchen alchemy, the ruby
red for which a century of glass painters strove.
And just over the bridge, past the petrol station
offering sundae dishes and tumblers, stands the house
where three hundred years ago lived Henry Gyles
'the famousest painter of glass perhaps in the world'.

A life given to the search for a lost secret,
his new stain turning to the colour of old blood,
the recipe for ruby glass elusive, expensive,
anxiety making his heart heavier, pocket lighter.
'I voided two rugged stones,' he wrote, *'which made
me piss as red as claret wine.'* In his garden, planting rose
and periwinkle, my friends dig up the crucibles in which
he mixed enamels. This spring they find fragments
of human bone and a Roman glass, unbroken.

He knew that there existed *'a most delicate
flaming red'.* He measured tincture, built a furnace,
fluxed enamels, layering silver onto white glass
but daily painted sundials for twenty shillings each;
the hound chasing the hare, an hour glass trickling,
ita vita. Still he mixed, stained, fired and found finally
the brilliant copper ruby with which he tinted the best houses
in Yorkshire: till the first sash windows slammed shut
and winning only church commissions, he died penniless.

Old glass weeps in the sun. Heat draws a breath
and each greenish pane, like a spadeful of riverwater
furnaced in air, each frame of ripple and bubble,
melts a little, runs, sinks into the lead and stone
that binds it. Old glass, buried in mud. Now she has
uncovered the whole thing, dated it, cleaned a section.
Simple glass, no fine brushwork, the plain colour red.
There must be two thousand pieces here, she thinks,
putting it all together would take time.

The lines quoted are from Henry Gyles' letters
to Ralph Thoresby (1658-1725), antiquarian,
topographer and good friend.

Mansize

Now you aren't here I find
myself ironing linen squares,
three by three, the way
my mother's always done,
the steel tip steaming over your
blue initial. I, who resent
the very thought of this back-breaking
ritual, preferring radiator-dried
cottons, stiff as boards, any amount
of crease and crumple to this
soothing, time-snatching, chore.

I never understood my father's trick,
his spare for emergencies, but was glad
of its airing-cupboard comforts often enough:
burying my nose in it, drying my eyes
with it, staunching my blood with it,
stuffing my mouth with it. His expedience,
my mother's weekly art, leaves me
forever flawed: rushing into newsagents
for Kleenex, rifling your pockets in the cinema,
falling on those cheap printed florals,

when what I really want is Irish linen,
shaken out for me to sink my face in,
the shape and scent of you still warm
in it, your monogram in chainstitch
at the corner. Comforter, seducer, key witness
to it all, my neatly folded talisman,
my sweet flag of surrender.

Cornwall, 1949

In Charlestown Bay the sea lapped in like milk,
creamy with china clay. The beach a still small shell
at the end of a dusty street, curled up in the sun.

You crossed the country on your fiery Norton,
she was a crab on your back and her flowery dress flew,
all day long summer beat your hearts together.

And in the deepest bowl she cracked two eggs
first of the new days, fresh laid: war was over,
this sponge was lighter than any they had known.

In Truro shopkeepers shook out clean blinds like flags,
you chose ripe plums under their stripey shield and
later buried the dull stones in warm sand.

But knowing they'd never grow green you climbed
to the tiny church's salty heights, your lips parched,
your eyes aching, looking so hard for Lyonesse.

Bathers, 1930

(from a photograph by George Hoyningen-Huene)

Staring so intently out to sea
they do not hear the stealthy camera
click like a key in a lock.

His hair is thick, sticky with salt.
Her hair is shingled. Their skins take a dip
in June sunlight. The air, the mood is blue.

The rest is out of focus; an ocean corrugates
and concertinas, the wind is a held breath,
the horizon too distant to believe in.

Their faces turned from us, they balance
on the edge of a narrow jetty. We look at them,
in black and white, from a long way off.

At Les Deux Magots

The bloom on the fruit is perfect.
His moist eyes are fixed on her.
As he hands her plums she thinks
he is the kind of man who'd kiss her
on the lips in friendship,
to whom she'd try to turn a cheek in time.
The way he gives me ripeness
when what I want is something raw.

An old memory makes the blood
rock in her veins: Ford, in the street,
face turned from her, arms filled with books,
the back of his crow-black coat resolute,
that moment, polished like a piece of bone.
Her thoughts are all crooked now,
her hands cold in their cotton gloves.
She takes the plums from him dumbly.

Sub Rosa

At Sissinghurst we are meant to gasp at
the borders. No one could fail to notice the
bulging veins of clematis shinning up and over
so much powdery red brick. Who could be
unimpressed by the swags of roses, carpets of camomile,
the best Sunday manners of it all? But we came
with our vague idea of Vita, Virginia, a friendship
under trees. Little of that left here, between
the roped-off library books, a shop exhaling pot-pourri,
scones leaning patiently on loaded plates.

We let ourselves out by the back gate, follow
the Lakeside Walk, till it collapses into nettles,
then fall down too, stretched out beneath
the cleanliness of trees, beside a scummy pool.
Water like pea soup, bright and green, on which
a single grebe is turning, leaving no wake.
Water where, weighed down with sorrows or stones,
the weed might part for you, close over your head silently.
Back in the garden the borders are busy with bees,
the air is humming with autorewinds, china and small change
chatter cosily, passion rots quietly under the rose.

Manuscripts

He opens an old chest on a world
of dead letters. Texas did not snap
up every single one and Ezra's
pencilled venom is sharp as citrus still,
a bile the years could not keep down.

A man from Sotheby's cruises
on the hard shoulder, past the angry
horns of stationary drivers, inside him
a moan of excitement answers them,
he puts down his exquisitely clad foot.

Dusted, authenticated, expensive papers,
in London his discoveries are up for grabs:
news of the mad and bad, how Tom
was only ever good for one thing, a desire
to have been, just once, dangerous to know.

·

Clare Leighton Packs a Bag, 1939

What I remember, she said, were her hands,
her huge hands, moving in the light.

She dug up light with a knife,
whittled shade to the bone,
heaped up shadow in the corners
of an English summer's day,
but everything was too black and white:
print on a page, a flickering screen,
the image she cut and bled onto paper,
reasons to fight, reasons to leave,
the wastepaper basket spilling over.

Maybe there was love, maybe discovery
in another country, a southern harvest
in another country. In London only
the grey stone, white air, grey stone
of a country waiting, its cornfields
ripening to the blare of poppies,
fireweed flaring in the cities.

Looking out then at all that snow
she knew paper was never as white
as this, no ink as black as her mood,
no wood as heavy, as hard, as this.
She carved out shade like a cancer,
slicing towards the light.

All Hallows

This is a day for souls.
Morning doused with air
that has rinsed itself,
wrung itself out over
cropped lands, picked lands, dug lands.
Autumn's over. Winter comes
in the first stiffening of grasses,
frost seasoning the land like salt,
a chill biting to the core of day.

The town's horizon blurs with
steam, smoke, mist, never resolving
quite the mesh of shiver and heat,
like looking at the world through tears.
Hot, salty tears can't melt the ice,
nor sluice his heart: but it's a comfort,
this light and water mixing,
on the day her soul walks out
over the fields to him.

Into the Blue

My daughter flashed her fins,
then swam past all precaution
into the blue milk of human kindness.

Sunlight struck her skin olivine, emerald,
all the secret shades of the deep,
colours we cannot guess at.

Sometimes her clean, even strokes
tangle in the long weed. She is surprised
by the slippery fronds the Japanese call Hair Plant.

But everything has its use. She cooks it,
serves it with a fish caught in her cupped hand:
Fugu, she cuts away its little poison sacs

with ten delicate nips of her pointed teeth.

Letter to Asa Benveniste. Good Friday 1990

(for Agneta Falk)

Dear Asa,

I hoped today I'd wake
and know I'd dreamt of you
last in thought sleeping,
first in thought waking,
but there was only an unaccountable
space and this blank page.

Where are you now?

We'll find you. There, in that photograph,
smiling from an ocean liner
as it pulls away from shore.
And here, in the scent we catch
from this bowl of apples,
sharp and green, rosy or russet.

Apples, *like two syllables of love.*

Apples which keep well,
lining our shelves like books,
letting us share a few
of their special names, private names,
holding the rest secret.

Apples, *like two syllables of love.*

The A Road

Driving out of town one summer evening
you said we'd take the backway home

and turned left out of terraced streets
onto a country lane as suddenly as

opening a blistered door on the *Secret Garden*:
at that moment in the book she knew happiness.

At that moment in the film we knew Technicolor,
at that moment on the road the West Country

blinded us with song. It meant we never found
a pub, it meant we passed Druid stones

and panoramic views heedlessly, the ripe air
was better than a stiff drink. But today,

on such an evening, you meet me at the station soberly.
Today, you drive too fast away from

the city, the hospital, our interlocking pasts.
Today, you say you can't remember which route

we took that night, that you only know
the A road and only ever have.

Clearer by Night

Arriving at dusk to wet roads
and the secret shapes of buildings
folded away in fields like sleeping beasts,
the wide sky closed from us and the horizon
declaring itself only by the false sunset
of a nuclear plant, clearer by night
in its halo of light, a small city on the edge
of black meadows, damp lanes,
on the edge of dreams.

Next day the scent of apples wakens me,
spilt from the trees, running indoors
to line the shelves six deep. No pesticides.
You'd rather risk the worm in the bud,
better to have them mealy, woolly on the tongue
to have to take a knife to them,
cut away the spot.

Medlars overflow each dish you find,
rotting to a delicious melt the way fear
dissolves now in this eastern morning light,
light that carries a bolt of iron,
harsh enough to reveal the lie of the land.

It's November and at Darsham station
a neglectful neighbour has fruit still left to pick.
The apples trees bow, rails stretch out in the sun.
The train greets a line of poplars, the faded
grass-coloured, honey-coloured clapboard
of Westerfield's deserted station house,

the patched and darned, tacked up,
made-to-do roofs of half a dozen barns.
I'm taking the path back to the capital,
where danger is only sometimes brightly lit,
where every apple is uniform, the horizon rarely glimpsed,
a large city that carries an edge of iron,
a large city at the heart of dreams.

CORNWALL COLLEGE
LIBRARY

Explaining Magnetism

Isolated here in the South, fiddling with British Rail
network charts, inhabiting the Underground plan, I learn
again how West means left and East means right.
I used to know that North was always straight ahead,
every map showed that cardinal point, a long feathered
arrow, a capital N. Whichever way I walked the land
restored itself to my own order: true North.

A compass only confused, school got in the way,
pointing at things you couldn't see,
explaining magnetism. In order to find out
I just went straight ahead and up there,
out of sight, was never isolated but isolate.
Down here, we move as one and jump like hamsters,
onto the Circle line. The names don't help much,
recalling that dull board game and me,

broke again, moving a top hat listlessly,
back and forth, left to right, round and round.

MOSS

St Brendan Explains to the Angel

You cannot understand this bog
how it seeps under the rock and broods,

how this hillside's green
forces me on from here, silent, fearful.

Nor how this hand of stone simmers
in a cool sea, great slabs of it to tear

a leather boat or barb an angel,
slapping at the waves, beaching the frail fish,

and the sun a crack in a stormy sky
where Lucifer always falls, is falling now.

A Boat to the Blaskets

His perfect English tells us he is Dutch,
and at his side the pale American
reads of the Marabar caves while
our little boat strokes a calm sea.
The quiet passage to a steep green island
where we step through daisies, driving the sheep
before us, to stand in the ruined houses,
and I want that face to be yours Peig.

Under the cliff we test the clear May water
with tiny cries, brave runs into the cold
which carries a fulmar, a gannet, a gull.
With our eyes we comb the bay for seals or leave
the hot white sand, picking like crabs along
the crumbling path to find above the ruined houses
two larks turning in the glassy air,
and I want to hear Tomas's foot on the soft grass.

The ferry is an hour late returning,
and we are beached on the slippery quay like shells,
or strangers, glad of this clumsy company
as we stare at the ruined houses, silently.
We didn't see tall waves, a mad black sea,
the mist that must have filled the stones like mortar,
those broken nets. Only an empty picture frame,
a small carved bed, a hearth of cold ashes.

Kerry Blue

A slatey smoke-backed creature,
lifting her delicate head
to the lavender sky.

Under molten clouds
she is fading violets,
or the dusty bloom on a damson.

Shaking her sea-coloured
coat till it shines
she might vanish with the mist,

leaving only her song,
a full green note on salt air.

Fabricio Spinola Flees from Ireland. 1588

A bank of licorice cloud threw wind and rain
and slammed the strand with waves all day. Tonight
high tide drew up a hundred crabs, a calf, a doll.

In such a storm the *Girona* settled down.
Gulls cast shrouds of mewing over the dead,
the broken boat oozed pearls amongst the rocks.

For weeks the sea breathed silver, gold and bone,
the flash of fins now dulled their eyes, they spread
fine nets at the water's edge and prayed.

Spinola lay with his ship in his arms
and on islands of weed his ring floated in,
No tengo mas que dar te, I have nothing more to give thee.

But he left his mark in hair, eye, a salamander
bloody with rubies, and gold, deep in the sand,
where digging for lug we long for doubloons.

Crossmaglen

Finger on catch: rifle – radio –
my job's to follow headlamps cut a track
and if they stop, I start. Rabbits.

From here I cannot see their tremble,
was never close enough to smell the fear.

Long nights I've sewn the pelts together,
slept under cover of their empty skins,
the ticking of those hearts is history.

1847

Ma's face is black with hair
her hands are paws.
She does not know me anymore.

Nights toss us cruelly.
Afraid I'll no more wake
I sit stony.

What knots my belly now's
not hunger. Anger.

In Liverpool ships gob us up.
We rot, we scatter.
The quays are maggoty with us.
We do not matter.

Vanished Lives

If we have no God, then we have ancestors.
She has lifted leather ledgers larger than herself,
printed soft warm thumbs on each curled corner,
and back she goes through a century and a half to 1837,
the last full stop.

A roll of names that
sent her to wet gravestones, her fingers feeling
for their vanished lives, but all is blurred here,
made less distinct by granite, slate or mossy characters.
And the other side is darker still:

blight that rotted fields
and emptied cottages, the crowded quay, the salt-rinsed boat,
a letter home. No records kept in spiny copperplate,
no cross to show that's where they've been,
only a face that's handed down and on,
glimpsed in a glass dark: Brigid McTighe, her mark.

Letters from Ireland

No hay has been saved.
The apple trees were bared
by an early east wind.
On one of the few fine days
with sea, high windows, Californian
skies, a blue tractor is mowing
the acres of lawn and
salmon pinks our plates.

Your uncle is in hospital.
Hong Kong does not need
our soft leathers and
the tannery has closed.
I've written to Nike and
Clarkes and returned the car.
Outside, the cattle lie down
in the fields and
it looks like rain.

Have you ever been to Greenland?
I have some notion of air,
or space or light,
I want a narrow bed,
a drying wind to pin my shirt on.
Wherever I go next
I'll send a postcard.

Currency

Driving from Derry to Donegal
my purse tries to hold
too many kinds of currency,

the radio flits between stations:
new songs, old stories, ads to cure calf sickness,
the endless bulletins of battle.

Reports from Kuwait cannot yet list the dead.
Breda Power imagines the Six out walking.

You drive. We stop and walk. You drive
and this could be freedom, something like

the tiny wake of sand my boots will leave
in tubes, on buses, in offices back home.

Last night the burst of shots we heard
went, unexplained, into the stars.

Today, on battlements at Doagh, moss grows,
mild water surrounds us, wind rocks the trees
and this could be peace, something like

this uneasy truce of figures in a landscape,
the radio making fiction of us all.

Casey, Cullen, Ward and McKeogh, 1969

4 walls and a roof.
Out on the edge of Europe,
here in the heart of England.

A bit of fishing and telly,
a bit of snooker and telly.

Lifting rocks from the land,
carrying hods in the city:
an open sky, a sodium street.

4 walls and a roof.
Out on the edge, here in the heart.

Casey, Cullen and Ward, 1999

4 walls and a screen.
Out on the edge of Europe,
here in the belly of England.

A bit of fishing and the Internet,
a bit of pool and MTV.

Selling off pieces of land,
playing Ftse in the City:
an open sky, a sodium street.

4 walls and a screen.
Here on the edge, out in the heart.

Moss

Your grandmother's castle is
a black and white photograph curling
in the hand's heat, a ruined tower
in the stranger's field. And on the door
your initials, carved in the heart of youth
are not even a speck in the picture's grain.

I'll go there someday. Pull back the barbed wire,
or set the chairs tumbling in the landlord's house
like some technicolored scene from *The Quiet Man*,
tossing my hair like a heritage, accent all wrong.

I'll go there someday find the approach too hard,
the bramble thick and high, the road unmarked,
the tower so softened by moss it's vanished utterly
slipped back into the land, like the language you left.

THE FUTURE MEMORY

'It's a poor sort of memory that only works backwards', the Queen remarked.

LEWIS CARROLL: *Alice Through the Looking Glass*

I began to perceive death in the most mundane of circumstances. Being photographed felt like being shot: it still does.

JODIE FOSTER

This is the use of memory:
For liberation – not less of love but expanding
Of love beyond desire, and so liberation
From the future as well as the past.

T.S. ELIOT: *Little Gidding*

Net and River

The old bus, nose to the road like a dog,
takes them all the way to the village
with its one shop and shining river.

The net she picks is green, uncertain
on its skinny pole as she dips it
back and forth, between the weeds,
over the stones and catches a fish.

A fish. A flicker and jump in water,
in air: a flash like memory itself.

Watching its ugly gasp for life,
the river fall from its back in tears,
the unkind swat of its head on stone,
she has to drop it back again

and let the waters close, the ripples spread
wide and wider till they can't be seen,
till the lip of deepest water stops its trembling.

Transubstantiation

Is the residue of the person transferred then,
transfixed by rays of the sun?

The camera steals the soul.

She'd like to think that whiteness
in the picture's grain's some essence
flit from darkness. That he'd be there,
embossed on light like the host she'd swallow
in the days when she could swallow it.

Eat me! Drink me! to be small again,
untroubled by the easy miracle of that word,
not hearing the shutter close against the light.

Wonderland

'Down, down, down. Would the fall
never come to an end?'

LEWIS CARROLL

The dark cloth in his hands,
then over his head, his
own breath warm about him.

She in a box: shadow and light
and like no trapped thing,
bumping at the frame, blind,

but solemn, her seven years
above ground childishly bright
and only her sleep to be plundered.

Shot

I stand on the grid and wait.
He says they'll turn the air vent on,
just think of something sad,
then something funny.
That napalmed child running,
the day Mr President was killed,
Woody Allen's trial...I say
but Geez, they haven't happened yet.

He wants to have it look authentic.
He needs some shake, tremble, desire.
I say this is not a problem,
this is the very opposite of a problem.
I throw back my head, they turn on the fan,
we do it, we make it, we shoot.

Stills

The room is a well of silence.
Mirrors are turned to the wall,
in case the soul, barbed like a fish,
should slip unseen under the silver
trapped forever on its final journey.

He has all of your shades in this box
was the Chief's cry: and we're to believe,
so Frazer tells us, that those simple – yes –
souls scrambled, fearful, their scattering
an anthropological pattern on a glass plate.

This one's for the hacks.
Romance, set down in black and white
in which you cannot smell his halitosis,
nor feel the blemish of her temper:
an air-brush clears up pits and pocks.

In this, *Last of her Tribe*,
the Clearances are a jagged emptiness
in her face. Roosevelt records her end
even as he orders it. Prescience.
Call her *last* and she will be.

Focus, block, crop, the sacred red lamp,
the dark, dark room. This is the murdered boy
and this the missing girl. Here is the pool
in which the young man gazed, silver,
so still, you can no longer hear the echo.

Echolalia

His version, his vision,
of the way the world works
is like those lightning moments
when a voice, a face, a street corner
from thirty years ago suddenly recurs,
raw as a cut. You wonder then
if the view is still the same,
the sun just clearing the chimneys
and the oak shape-shifting
all the long afternoon, and you know
that it can't be, will always be,
forgetting, for that instant,
which end of the telescope
you're looking through.

KISSING A BONE

History

It's only a week but already you are slipping
down the cold black chute of history. Postcards.
Phonecalls. It's like never having seen the Wall,
except in pieces on the dusty shelves of friends.

Once I queued for hours to see the moon in a box
inside a museum, so wild it should have been kept
in a zoo at least but there it was, unremarkable,
a pile of dirt some god had shaken down.

I wait for your letters now: a fleet of strange cargo
with news of changing borders, a heart's small
journeys. They're like the relics of a saint.
Opening the dry white papers is kissing a bone.

What Every Woman Should Carry

My mother gave me the prayer to Saint Theresa.
I added a used tube ticket, kleenex,
several Polo mints (furry), a tampon, pesetas,
a florin. Not wishing to be presumptuous,
not trusting you either, a pack of 3.
I have a pen. There is space for my guardian
angel, she has to fold her wings. Passport.
A key. Anguish, at what I said/didn't say
when once you needed/didn't need me. Anadin.
A credit card. His face the last time,
my impatience, my useless youth.
That empty sack, my heart. A box of matches.

Protagonist

He rehearses the station: knows the release
of a brake's steady application,
sweat, anticipation's dying fall,
the mercy of a busy platform,
shadows scattering in the ticket hall,
then the one shadow.

From a window open to the sea,
a torn's dark underlife is undertow,
its evening rope of stars and strangers,
hauls him in, silvery, slow, down

down, till he's shown how and where
the thing they've kept hidden,
too sophisticated now even to tick,
might explode into life, or worse,
that other trick. He never meant to do harm,
wanted only to keep their hearts warm.

Going the Distance

He fills her glass. She raises it.
The nearest he comes to telling her
is here in this silence. With the weight
of his life backed up behind him like a truck,
in the time it takes her heart to skip a beat,
he travels the length of that old road again.

The dream of leaving: nipping out for fags,
a box of matches, never looking back.
Returning to the island after years away
only the coinage would feel strange to him,
crenulations beaten smooth by distance,
shifting in his hand like the sea, whose dazed
blue space, calm and flat beneath him, is
the Atlantic's slow unfurling of its flag.

She drains her glass and lowers it.
The waiter clearing dishes from the table
is tender and efficient as a priest.
They settle up. She opens a door on London.
He closes it. They move into the crowd.

The Line

A heavy linen cloth,
her dress of shooting stars,
the brittle blue of spring,
his sodden woollen shirt.

The peg becomes a pen,
fills the line with cursive,
a changing word in wind,
love or *duty* or *life*

The Message

How, at an open window the wind
filled a shirt with the shape of his body,
pressed it flat as an idea again.

Then, turning back the covers one still night
she found a bat in her bed, cupped it,
flung its small warmth into the sky.

But, the need for a cigarette
was the need to press hard on the wheel
of his Zippo: pain, ignition.

So, when the parcel came she wasn't surprised
that all his curls spilled out,
clipped, abundant and with no message.
Somewhere, his head was cool and clear and free.

Heat

Summer swells like a fruit.
Long evenings hang
the way small insects hug a storm lantern.
Already we have forgotten about covers,
know that this will be called *that summer*.

Staring across fields to where
water breaks this land in two
we cannot see it gleaming,
even under full moon.
Intention and purpose
are hidden among long grasses,
the low coughs of sleeping beasts.

How to peel the truth from this,
expose the ripeness of the moment,
juice in our mouths and our hands still clean.

Foreign Correspondent

We are inventing for ourselves a story.
The other life. A narrative that frets and stumbles
yet moves along at such a pace, I'm winded.

Water keeps the distance words try to close.

A peace-keeping force means soldiers in,
then soldiers out. The arms' embargo's off.
A meteor falls, another sign to read.

I do, I read and read, your words, the heavens'.

Remember, this is the oldest of games:
paper, scissors, stone,
the power of hands pretending.

Does It Go Like This?

The day seawater swilled my lungs
he guided me back without ever once touching me.
Lying on shingle, like the two halves
of the equator, I thought my heart would burst,

not knowing in which element it drowned.
Now, two hundred miles from him, beached
on larkspur, lark song, I struggle to remember
something I used to know: *did it go like this? Like that?*

How did it start? At Capel-y-Ffin what rises
from dark red dirt, what's netted now
is flotsam of sheepskull filleted by maggots,
a dead pony's ribs taut as ship's rigging

and here, where a draught of summer
rinses tired skin with cuckoo syncopation,
with percussion of bees, old fears rush in
fierce as a tide. Blood, not birdsong

pulses at my ear: the strong cross-currents
that beat in these shallows, the meat
and bone under bright meadow grasses,
the heart's tricky business of staying alive.

Remember the day we saw divers trawl the Thames
heavy with rosaries of gas and rope,
angels with black rubber wings and serious faces
dropping through mist and into the deep, like psalms?

What is that tune whose words I try to catch
Does it go like this? Like this? How does it begin?
I dredge up only the middle, a jaded chorus,
of a song I used to know right through by heart.

Up on the Roof

You wonder why it is they write of it, sing of it,
till suddenly you're there, nearest you can get
to flying or jumping and you're alone, at last,
the air bright. Remembering this, I go
with my too-light jacket up to the sixth floor,
out onto the roof and I freeze under the stars
till he comes with my too-heavy jacket, heavier
and heavier, as he tries to muffle my foolishness.
A blanket on a fire (he says) and it's true
I am left black, bruised a little, smouldering.

You can sit with a book up there and reel in
life with someone else's bait. You can let your eyes
skim the river, bridges, banks, a seagull's parabola.
At night, you can watch the sky, those strange galaxies
like so many cracks in the ceiling spilling secrets
from the flat above. You can breathe. You can dream.

But he turns to me, as you'd coax a child
in the back of a stuffy car: *we could play I-Spy?*
I look at the black and blue above and the only
letter I find is 'S'. I cannot name
the dust of starlight, the pinheaded planets,
but I can join the dots to make a farming tool,
the belt of a god: all any of us needs is work,
mystery, a little time alone up on the roof.

The Spoils

But when it came to records
I just said *take the lot.*
They're like a map of where
it all went wrong, *tender, true,*
the long and winding road.
Not much on anger till I saw
her hold the hammer, remembered
Ella, Bessie, Billie, *sad, blue.*

Heart

(for my father)

Your heart, like an old milk tooth
hanging by a thread: a strength we'd test
with temper, trust, the exquisite tug of truth.

Enlarged, we knew what that meant.

And now, I want your big heart here,
to chart its absences: the yellow stream
of bitterness, the silver river of malice,
the empty shore of Lake Envy,

all the landscapes it had never known
and all the different countries it contained.

Dark

I lit up only slowly,
coming back to life when
it was clear you could not.
My veins thick as cords,
my skin paler. In the year
I grew old my heart rustled,
thin as cigarette paper.

But one of us had to get
warm again. I partied, I fucked,
I lay awake through the smallest
hours watching headlamps sweep
the ceiling like hands of a clock.

You told me how at night they stable
the trains, leaving them snug
in the long tunnels.
So, tell me what they dream of,
humble there, in the dark.

Blood

(for Simon Dennis)

Something leaked into his blood
the way he entered mine
and never left. Old friendship,
where love leaves its watermark
under the years and all
the *keep meaning to*s fall away
to reveal a life maybe you knew,
maybe you didn't, a voice
saying something, a hand,
his, mine,
and how it was taken.

The Captain's Inventory

There were rooms he never entered:
study, living room,

this one, facing south, where the swallows'
return is a gift of purity, measure, hope.
Or the cellar, locked against memory,
tools and turps, earth and darkness.

The kitchen shrank to a toaster and
down through the mansion of his heart
you could hear the echo of feet, slamming
of doors, till everything slowed to this:
chair, bottle, view of the harbour.

The Celestial Announcer

On the day that you hear
the station announcer
call out the towns and villages
of your life, as if she'd read
the very chapters of your soul,
that knowing way she has of saying *Halifax*,
the way she skirts around poor rainy *Manchester*,
and jumps to the conclusion now of *Luddenden* –
with its ghost of a station
and dream of Branwell drunk under the stars –
and all the big and little places
you have ever been, would like to go,
chanted, charted,

well, then you realise it's time to change
your mind, ticket, journey,
point of departure,
Estimated Time of Arrival
and know that she will lend you wings
for those golden slippers, milk and honey,
bread, roses and a brand new map.

Home

The past
as night is,
pitch, peat,
as blood is
when the heart stops.

Dancing at Oakmead Road

Sometimes I think of its bright cramped spaces,
the child who grew there and the one we lost,
how when we swept up for its newest lover
the empty rooms were still so full of us.

The honeyed boards I knew would yet hold close
our dusts, some silver from my father's head,
the resin of the wood would somehow catch
in patina the pattern of his tread.

That time in the back room, laughing and drunk,
Geraldo and his orchestra, a tune
that had you up and waltzing and me quiet,
my throat so achey at the sight of you,

glimpsing for a second how it might have been
before his mouth went down on yours, before
the War, before the children broke into
the dance, before the yoke of work. Before.

Gone

You were only a bag of soft stuff
but I imagined you like a nut,
your brain beginning to pack itself
around the kernel that is me.
My limpet, my leech,
my little sucker-in of blood.
Gone. Sometimes I think we know
of nothing else, lost loves, lost lives,
the hopeless benediction of rain.

Freight

I am the ship in which you sail,
little dancing bones,
your passage between the dream
and the waking dream,
your sieve, your pea-green boat.
I'll pay whatever toll your ferry needs.
And you, whose history's already charted
in a rope of cells, be tender to
those other unnamed vessels
who will surprise you one day,
tug-tugging, irresistible,
and float you out beyond your depth,
where you'll look down, puzzled, amazed.

Biting Point

In a borrowed car I am following instruction.
Reverse the car around this corner and pull up
safely. It is uphill, uneven, blind,
the road is busy. I look back. I move slowly.
I look back. Under my baggy shirt
another person stirs, shrugging my skin
like too many bedclothes, impatient.

In a moment I am going to say stop
and I want you to stop, under full control,
as if in emergency. My feet stamp the floor.
My daughter bangs crossly. *Stop.*
I have stopped. I have looked back.
I have looked hard in the mirror.
The car hasn't even stirred the gravel.

Good, says my examiner, *I shan't ask you to do that again.*
Outside a Birch lets go of leaves,
I think of my girl and me, each in our carriage,
like Russian dolls. *Drive on,*
the stranger's voice commands. And we do.

Into Holes

When she was born they gave us
a pair of old sheets
to cut up and sew for the cot.
Gone into holes and golden,
where their bodies' heat had broken
to sweat, the end of sweat, raggedy
where the washing, lying, washing,
wore them and wore them again.

Now that a torn sheet's too wide
for the narrow beds they keep,
and the weight of a loved one's breath
suddenly too much to bear,
I cannot take a scissors
to this, the map of their happiness
where the hushing, laughing, hushing,
warmed us and warms us again.

The True Ark

If you joined them,
the pieces of the true ark
would make a fleet,
their sails a white road
from here to the horizon.

Stepping from boat to boat,
a frog among waterlilies,
you might peer below deck
and that sharp stink rising
would reveal the lair of
dodo or phoenix or sphinx.

At night, becalmed, you wonder
at the voice calling 'Time!'
as the sails come down and the vessels
break up before your very eyes,
lodging themselves in museums, stories,
as a splinter in your waiting palm.

Talks About Talks

There's memory, there's truth
and there's the way the machine works:
a splice, a little oil,
a steady hand with the two wires.
I could find a story in it for you,
though it would beggar belief
and you'd hate the ending, or feel
you'd heard it before, it being
not new but one of the six tales
that roam the world in search of a teller.

There's future, there's past
and there's politics:
a speech, a little gossip,
a shakey hand obeying a shaking head.
I could find meaning in it for you,
though it mightn't ring true
and you'd hate the translation, or feel
you'd do better yourself
with a bulky dictionary and body language.

There's talk, there's silence
and there's the way you sit now:
a table, a little fidgeting,
the steady ticking of an old, sad clock.
I could find history in it for you,
though it mightn't be news
and you'd hate the film version, or feel
you'd lived it already, if only
you could remember when and where and why.

Making Tea in the Corridors of Power

We all knew that disease idled in the water tank
but only she could say who favoured a Hobnob
and from whom the Nice biscuits were hidden.

Turner's was black with very little sugar
but Bates wanted lightener *swirled like a cloud*.
No sweeteners. No sweeteners of any kind.

Bailey's came in a china cup:
the spoon's *tinkle, tinkle* pleasured him,
the vibration, the promise.

After late meetings there was a shuffle, a scuttle
over stale crumbs and in the mornings she could
smell them. Once, she even glimpsed a scaley tail.

Night Driving

Across the Pennines maybe, at first frost,
when your headlamps make milky the way ahead,

or approaching Toronto at 4.00 a.m.
when stars lie scattered on the still lake,

driving fast, the windows pulled down,
to let the night winds steady your hands

you're tuned into strange stations
playing old hits you wish you didn't know.

Turning a dial fills the air with static:
oceans, the blueness of night

and you own the road, the country.
The radio speaks only to you.

Keith Jarrett

Riding that piano as if he's fused somehow,
as if the beast of it rising under his hands
might toss him into the air,

its shimmying flank, its hungry mouth,
that tender moment of patience or trickery
before the heels, horns and meat of it

rear into his ears, nose, mouth
and he sings, hums, stamps,
he whispers, pleads, croons,

reining in, easing, taming finally
the wail of the earth, the song of sex,
the long salt sigh in each of us.

The Bridge

In Africa, under the dark impossible
bridge that links before the War with after,
he gathered the fallen avocado
for squadron leaders who remembered
pyramids of unblemished flesh in Fortnums.

Black and blue, purple as cardinals,
later he carried them back
from occasional trips to London,
his thumb pressing a rough skin, for give,

making up rules for a spell
in the airing cupboard, or nestling
in a bowl of rosy apples. Delicious bruise,
stone-hearted, leathery ark of dreams.

Now, when even the corner shop
displays the burnished fruit,
his memory of war, distant, green,
begins to turn darker and ripen.

Last Hours in the City

The yellow trams glide past like stray cartoons,
carriage by carriage stripe the street with a story.

On Kruisstraat the man in the blue anorak
tests words on us that the wind cuts up.

Maybe he offers religion or needs money
but all night rain erases his shadow,

and all the other shadows of trains or stories
that polish the tramline's reading of this city.

In the morning, through his open window,
traffic noise will ripen like a field of wheat,

the falling weight of afternoon recalling
prairies, home, a golden square before him,

no shade anywhere, then dusk again,
like hunger, eating into night.

Pathetic Magic

At the door
the love we want to offer
gathers itself.

Safe Home, Take Care,
Good Luck, God Bless,
a rabbit's foot.

Nothing saves us
from the boat tossed over,
a leaf in storm,

like my heart
turning now,
as darkness takes you,

and somewhere
a door slams,
long, long into the night.

The Shape of Things

You gather-in mood, tone, a look,
working over the words,
as if a good pummelling ever made
better sense of anything.
Wrung out, hung up, the shape of things
is blindingly, dully, different.

Between even the oldest friends
Doubt hoists its tattered flag
and tiny moments blow away,
are slapped around in storm:
you have to tear it down, or wait
and trust for days of stillness, happiness.

The Discovery

I am the man who discovered Australia,
at 12 noon, one late Indian summer.
Thumbing through my atlas for the farthest
outpost of the known universe
what stopped me was that glorious shape,
I entered there. The coral reefs,
the wide interior, that harbour
with the soaring wings of song:
I was the man who woke to find himself
on the bridge of a violin,
music in his ears, vibration, unholy joy.

Ice

At Richmond the ice is crooning
under the tentative weight of sticks and pebbles
we lob and slide across a frozen pond. A marvel.

Strangers exchange troubled smiles,
never dreaming before that ice had its own song,
a dull forgiving echo for those who stand at the side

watching for cracks, those who don't know how to skate,
and those who try to read the hieroglyphs
under the soft muzz of scurf the dancers heels kick up.

Walking

(for Miroslav Mandic and Jo Shapcott)

Miroslav Mandic is walking.
From Hölderlin to Rimbaud he journeys
with solitude, a walking stick, sweat.
It was the walking stick and me walking,
the two of us like waves.
It was the walking stick and me walking,
homelessness and I.
In villages where they don't know
what poetry is, what art is, he explains
his walking, he explains poetry:
he tells them it is like love,
he tells them it is sweat.
I read his work in clumsy translation,
the road opened me, he writes.
Can he mean that? Just that?

Miroslav Mandic is walking
from Rimbaud to Blake, not to honour their work,
not because they are important but to celebrate
poetry. Sometimes wind blows colder than rain,
sometimes milk curdles in his knapsack,
but it is nothing, none of it matters,
and it is everything. *Isn't language also walking?*
Isn't walking also a form of writing?
Isn't the road the greatest, the most beautiful
building in the world?

Miroslav Mandic is walking.
At Bunhill Fields, near Blake's grave,
on London grass, his walking stick
becomes a huge pen, forms the word *i*,
in his country this means *and*.
And each footfall is an and, and each footfall
a small connecting word, a conjunctive,
a continuance, and, and, and.
He walks in order to turn every there into here
and he tells us it is like love,
he tells us it is sweat,
he tells us it is poetry, and

131

More Than Twice the Speed of Sound

Some, remembering other blasts, threw themselves
to the ground. Sheep ran in fear and angry farmers
later said they lost their young that day but our small faces,
turned upwards to the bright, white, empty sky,
were wordless, only the baby jiggling in her pram,
bonneted, cosseted, spoke for us all: *again, 'again, 'gain.*
Windows shattered, glass sprayed like a fountain, splinters
splashing and rolling, rolling to far corners, where today
they surface sometimes between Desirées and King Edwards.

If I could gather them up, each sharp and dangerous fragment,
and piece it all together, make a grouting of my love,
if I could find in it a vivid, extravagant story,
new-ancient like the frescoes of Ravenna,
if I could restore each grimy window-pane, would you,
could you, see it all differently, our wondering faces,
the sound barrier simply waiting to be broken?

NEW POEMS

Our Lives and Ourselves

Mam, I want you to know
I made this the old way
with paper and pencil,
rough copy, fair copy,
a child at my elbow
and not enough sleep.

I wanted to tell you
the parlour still smells
of snuff and of polish,
of musk roses, soot,
the chill Northern wind
and the dampness of spring.

On Sundays while Nellie
and Clem are at Chapel,
I sit setting down here
my heart's smallest secrets,
in ways I could never,
when life was your shroud.

A mother, a daughter,
the rough and fair copies,
I never could tell you
our own little story
of soot, of musk roses,
our lives and ourselves.

I want you to know, Mam,
it's your hands I gaze at
spread over these letters,
as if to protect them
from words and from meaning,
from something as simple

as just making sense.
This silence between us,
has made the keys blurry,
the way this 'g' trembles
on a word I once fought
that now fits like a glove.

Clitheroe
1937

Sexton and Merwin, 1968

(from a photograph by Jill Krementz)

In this picture of Anne Sexton
she is asking something of W.S. Merwin
and cigarette smoke makes
the smallest cloud between them.
See how her long legs tie themselves,
how her hand grips the tenderness at her throat
as if she would grasp it, wrench out
that damned voice box: *Here! You want it?*
Take it! It's yours. All yours.
And what would it be like, that tiny coffin,
that treasure chest? Open her book. Look.

The Blackbird Whistling

I do not know which to prefer,
The beauty of inflections,
Or the beauty of innuendos,
The blackbird whistling
Or just after.

            WALLACE STEVENS,
            'Thirteen Ways of Looking at a Blackbird'

It is the second before the bow finds the string,
twilight, dusk, the hour of benedictions,
seen from a distance, a candle's swift guttering,
that sharp intake of breath, your indecision.

It is the moment when the moon obscures the sun,
the long steep fall of a pebble down a well,
watched from afar, the splash of tears on stone.
In Antarctica you can hear each snowflake fall

but this space is the pause before the applause,
or the interval coughs, a bewilderment
of pain and joy, anticipation, fear, relief. It is eleven
on the eleventh of the eleventh, the memory of grief.

It is the small wish of his ashes as they slip into the wind,
it is that moment when the bow finds the string.

A Blank Film

On Assateague and Chinquateague
the wild ponies we watched for kept hidden
and the astonished faun who came upon us,
as we listened to the strange songs of strange birds,
was a blank when the film came back.

The Cape Henlopen lighthouse sought
through narrow lanes, quaint on my tea towel,
had slipped under waves half a century before,
washing up here tonight, in those moments,
when questions go unanswered,
when eyes open on darkness, emptiness, silence.

Spreading the tea towel to dry
I could recite from it for you, the names of all
the lighthouses of the Eastern Atlantic seaboard,
Sandy Hook, Castle Hill, Brant Point,
West Quoddy Head, the Isle of Shoals.

Their lights are a stranger's cry across the water,
a gasp or a sigh, breaking up ice,
each beam like turning a page,
flooding the darkness for a single moment
and then another moment and another.

1943

(Shostakovitch:Symphony No.8 in C Minor)

Earth, and then, a handful of glass, sharp,
the silver thread of firstmorninglight.
Early hours. In the early hours,
when they'll come, or when they might come,
or when they do. In the shadows, in the half-light,
in the small hours, first ice, fear and its children,
the wet birch leaves slapping the window.
The mind turns against day. Against day.
The land, dark under rain, snow, heavy skies,
the land itself then closes like a door.

Ten Letters, A Something Z Something

He always grasps the wrong end now,
searching for a light but almost had it then,

the memory of something all gone up in smoke,
and tries again. She wants to fill him in

the way they used to crack the Cryptic. Four letters,
another country, they do things differently there.

She turns his cigarette around, strikes a match.
Now he's the anagram she cannot solve.

Invitations on the Mantelpiece

The position of the partners to each other should be close, so that
both move as one person. If you look at the perfect dancing
couple in profile, no space will be visible between them.
VICTOR SILVESTER
Modern Ballroom Dancing (1932)

Stiff white card and gold block.
Cocktails. Black tie. RSVP.
The mysterious shorthand of an adult world.
Dinner and Dance brought babysitter,
anxiety in an evening dress,
tissue paper on a nicked chin,
the unifying struggle of the bow-tie,
two pairs of scuffed shoes by morning,
and on the table, a twist of paper napkin,
a tiny boat, a cargo of sequestered petits-fours.

Then, at a family wedding,
well-matched in our awkwardness,
my teenage cousin and I
stumble through smoky music
till, slippery as eels,
we find the hidden stream
and for a few moments,
another element, another life.
In our sweaty clutch at joy
here was a feeling swift and strange
that we could neither name nor own.
A shiver of raw life, fear,
desire and despair united us,
pierced us and passed from us
as we turned, golden, glistening,
back to the tables of bottles,
fag-ends and familiar faces.

I cannot dance upon my Toes –
No Man instructed me –
But oftentimes, among my mind,
A Glee possesseth me

An idea of passion lay in the shimmering,
reflective surface of a pair of dancing pumps.
'You should be able to see your face in it.'
I'd struggle to, gazing deep
as if that toecap was a crystal ball.
Shiny black. Liquid, midnight black.
The fruity black of the darkest sloe.
Quick, quick, slow black.

The bandleader's call for a Ladies' Excuse Me
lights a flare of intoxicated laughter
as unwilling, sheepish, delighted,
furious or resigned shapes
are pulled to the dance floor,
unspoken, unresolved or spontaneous quarrels,
bargainings and fancyings
all dragged into the light in that moment.
The one who says he cannot dance,
the gorgeous longed-for one
to whom she'd dared not speak,
the anxious one, the angry one,
the two women smiling shyly together.

Will you, won't you, will you, won't you,
will you join the dance?

Sugared-almond-pink, I have them still
that first pair of ballet shoes,
a shade I no longer care for,
even as I dress my daughter in it
and watch her become fairy,
giant, a blade of grass in wind.
A child whose whole body jived
before she could walk. A child
whose second word was *dance*,
whose first, sighed longingly,
chanted, meant the same thing:
hungry, hungry, hungry.

Just as once, flight cancelled,
we shared bottled water
with a group of Catalans
whose patience grew to fever,
as first fiddle, clapping, stamping,
then a wild wave of dancing
caught the party, splashing over
the Microsoft delegates, the listless children,
the Japanese rugby club –
the queerest collection of fish
found themselves dipping into that pool.
Until things drew to a dry conclusion:
fire regulations, obstruction of gangways, risk.

With the toot of the flute
And the twiddle of the fiddle-o
Hopping in the middle
Like a herring on the griddle-o...

It was the dance we did during washing-up.
A dance liable to slippage and breakage:
yellow cups, blue saucers, everything chipped.
Tea-towel on shoulder, a bulky form
turning precisely on delicate feet,
whooping up the suds to glittering froth,
Dad jigged down Sunday afternoons.

Saturday night in Seville,
a two-shows-a-night bar, seedy,
I should have known better,
waiting for Flamenco to begin.
The guitarist late, the dancer
a mask of fury, her crimson dress
flexing with heat and rage.
A small room, like the skin of a drum
and she, the beater.
When the musician arrived,
stared, shrugged, played,
her dance licked the walls of the bar.
The ones who'd nearly left,
the ones who'd drunk too much,
the ones who'd chosen the first bar they'd seen,
all sat like stones, as, to the deepest song of all,
she gave herself.

If I had reached to touch her molten dress,
my fingers still would bear the mark,
all the black same I dance my blue head off!

In the bright black of those shoes,
tap-tapping through the dance halls
of my seven-year-old dreams,
was the glitterball, the indigo air eddying,
lipstick, the creak of ice in gin.
The brittle black of patent leather
needed cream, a velvet cloth, elbow grease,
the oils of anticipation and affection.

'Ah now, my dancing days are over.'
Later still, in the bottom of the wardrobe
were the shoes, waiting to be found,
to push their toes up, up into the light.
When I lifted each one it was only
to be amazed at their weight, their unloveliness,
the heaviness of their history.
What were they but a pair of old shoes,
their insides dry and splintery, their faces dull
and what else was there to do
but find the jar, the cloth and begin again.

'You should be able to see your face in it,'
and now that I could no longer see his,
I might as well try to see my own.

In the long summer of growing up,
after 'A' Levels, before the world began,
we spent the tall nights walking, smoking, drinking.
A tight coil of friends I never see now,
sprung, as we are, into a wider cooler life.
West Country children, footloose, feckless,
dangerous in our innocence,
finding one night, in the lea of the Severn,
the ruined body of a grand hotel –
moonlight, the last guest to leave.
Inside, cheerful in our fearfulness,
we were washed with silence to find
a broken ballroom, half the floor gone,

carried out to line a study or light a fire:
the rest laid down in whorls and grain
the stories of the years before
and suddenly, over those footsteps,
under that all-seeing moon, we four danced.
What did we understand in that moment,
beside the long windows, open to deep waters?
O body swayed to music, O brightening glance,
knowledge that lies listless in the blood,
quietly, quietly till summoned.

Risk. To find again that slippery, delicious element
in which I neither swam nor breathed
but which felt as unlikely,
as utterly right, as sleep or air.
To move in it as if I owned it.
Sometimes I caught just the whiff of it.

Slovenia. 1991. Independence.
Border guards check passports and money.
My small brick of fresh banknotes,
exchanged an hour before in Trieste,
is spread out on the bullet-proof ledge
like mosaic, a cartoon strip, a line of flags.
For the first time these soldiers gaze down
at the new currency of their new country.
The notes stare back up at them,
a row of joyous signposts.
Slovenia. Slovenia. Slovenia. Wonder. Delight.

In those men, in those faces, in those seconds,
the bird of hope alights. Through the screens
we watch the notes detonate a small explosion of joy,
as two soldiers try on the feeling of freedom.
Clapping and twirling, arms linked, fluttering
paper money like a morris dancer's handkerchiefs,
like wings, they stamp and roar a wild saltarello
within that cage of glass and steel
and their spirits fly up, beating a way out
into the clear, June sky.

Remembering this, knowing moments when
the unknowable has danced into me, sends me
in search of this mystery. I scan my shelves.

Mr Victor Silvester, brilliantined elegance,
world champion ballroom dancer, 1923,
advises: *a dance a week*
keeps you healthy and sleek.

Mr Silvester, you did not come to class late,
your sheltering armpit wet and malodorous.
Mr Silvester, you did not squeeze too tight,
nor breathe your maggoty breath
on your partner's neck: your rictus smile,
your knife, like a glittering crescent moon
was hidden well. No *shining web* was there,
no *floating ribbon of cloth.* Just the same
something fast and furious takes hold.

Stiff white card and gold block.
Cocktails. Black Tie. RSVP.
All the mysterious shorthand of the adult world.
The anxious one, the angry one,
the two women smiling shyly together.
The toot of the flute, the twiddle of the fiddle-o.
Slipping like eels into a hidden stream.
The broken ballroom. Risk.
Hungry. Hungry. Hungry.
The knowledge that lies listless in the blood.
The unifying struggle of the bow-tie.
The oils of anticipation and affection.
Her molten dress. A small explosion of joy.
The new currency of a new country.

Zoology

At seventeen the girls get the canteen
and the boys the elephant house.

Our atlases are cheap hotelware on which
the bloodied shores of India or Africa

spring from congealed beans. We swill and stack.
Under trees, Paul scrubs the rough grey flanks

of docile beasts, tenderly lifts ears like barn doors,
like wings, and through the steam Anne and I can just see

Wendy trumpetting, a fallen angel, water spilling off
in great glorious showers. Guaranteed Unbreakable,

we swill and stack heavy white plates,
dreamy with a new world we know is ours.

An endangered species howls. The elephant, the boy,
the girls, the day, gather in their summer hours.

The Harrigan Sisters

In black and white you cannot see it:
the three different shades of red
that make up the curls of the Harrigan sisters,

Strawberry, copper, terracotta. Like leaves
they turned through the ballrooms of the Forties,
then turned again to motherhood, disappointment.

They shake their paintbox heads.
Not like that, not like that at all.
What do I know of the bombed city,

the vanishings, the unlit streets, the telegram.
If I look closely I can see the boxy tailoring,
the leg-of-mutton sleeve and dirndle waist

but not the colours of their lovely heads.
I cannot hear leaves dancing at the window,
nor smell the past burning.

Mirror

In my mother's house
is the friendly mirror,
the only glass in which I look
and think I see myself,
think, yes, that's what
I think I'm like,
that's who I am. The only
glass in which I look and smile.

Just as this baby smiles
at the baby who always
smiles at her, the one in
her mother's arms, the mother
who looks like me, who
smiles at herself in her
mother's mirror, the friendly
mirror in her mother's house.

But if I move to one side
we vanish, the woman I thought
was me, the baby making friends
with herself, we move to one side
and the mirror holds no future, no past,
in its liquid frame, only the corner
of an open window, a bee visiting
the ready flowers of summer.

The Weighing of the Heart

What does the heart weigh?
More than the pull of your small
hand on mine? More than your head's
light heaviness on my shoulder?

Under the tender pressure of sleep
my old wool jacket becomes
your memory of consolation, comfort,
that ancient sweetness of love and tweed.

Remembering this, watching you,
I lose my place entirely, not knowing
whose the head, whose the sleeve,
whose the big hand and whose the small.

The Ancients measured a good heart
against the slightest puff of down,
in the gleam and glitter of delicate scales.
Like Thoth, we watch and wait.

What does the heart weigh?
Less than your head's tiny burden,
for lighter than a feather is love
and this the Egyptians knew.

I'm Not in Love

Remember the boy with a glass in his hand?
How, one crack too many put him inside for life,
left Pete's heart puttering to a standstill.

All summer the jukebox gagged on 10cc. *It's because.*

You grew up to be a lawyer, Pete's dead
and here's that boy in a glossy mag; sad captive,
talking bird. *You'll wait a long time for me. You'll wait a long time.*

That summer had no shade but exams,
cutting a coolness from college to college,
and her face deep enough to drown in.

Now he starts his third degree, writing cramped,
a block of paper, narrow feint, margins.
He is trying to get that damn song out of his head. *It's because.*

The Route

Too late to trace the dangerous
turnings of his ear,
to read the corniche road
that marks a finger's tip,
to touch that palm
and see it all mapped out.
What brought me here? A voice,
the eye's steadfastness,
the arms' encirclement,
a car door's slam. The idea of loss.

December on the Northern Line

The flamenco of feet
frames days like cracks

in a long dark winter
through which we squeeze,

heads down. *Please don't
notice me. Please. Don't.*

A woman in the Underground
waiting for the gifts of Spring:

an extra hour of daylight,
violets on the barrow at Waterloo.

A Visit to the Optician

There's something in my light: interference, distortion,
the razzle-dazzle of a foreign station,
stars in my eyes, dust, tears. Tune me in.
Make contact – the way his handkerchief
briefly, famously, once cleared her misty vision.

I try to read but – kaleidoscope, stroboscope,
magic lantern – before my very eyes the world
breaks up. Words lose their pattern of
country, continent, ocean and scatter alphabets,
archipelagoes of loose language.

I'm not Saint Lucy, who tore out her eyes
the better to see. I will not be blinded by love,
you, the delusions of my age. Lend me some glasses.
Pass the telescope. I'll stuff these lenses in.
I will not miss the passing of this heavenly body.

Raft of Desires

(for Noel Connor)

It's the old, old story.
Warm wind on the night ferry,
a glass and a dark song,
let this be the one.

The path rising to meet me,
the wind always behind me,
a stroll and a dander
at the shining sea's edge.

And it's over, it's over,
over the water and over,
the life I once knew
and the life I have left.

The Playground

Last night my old headmaster
came visiting. Elderly, smiling,
he put his papery hand in mine.
Did he visit too the middle-aged
dreams of my class mates? Somewhere,
will we all line up on the asphalt?
The one who lost a sister to the drink,
the one who ate himself to freedom,
and all the ones I cannot name,
could never really name.
And will we go there again yesterday?
my young daughter asks hopefully
of the playground we left so recently,
the empty swings still moving to and fro
in the mild violet of the long afternoon.